How to TRAIN your PUPPY

- a READ-it-YOURSELF
Guide for KIDS

**Instructions & Illustrations
by
Catherine Maven, M.A.**

Text & Illustrations by Catherine Maven
Copyright © 2023

All rights reserved. This book or any portion thereof may not be reproduced or used in any manner whatsoever, in print or online, without the express written permission of the publisher except for the use of brief quotations in a book review.

NOTE: The material contained in this book is set out in good faith for general guidance and no liability can be accepted for loss or expense incurred as a result of relying in particular circumstances on statements made in the book.

First Printing: April 2021
ISBN: **978-1-990333-00-2**

Otter-Girl Press
Burlington, Ontario, Canada
https://sleepingcat.wixsite.com/ottergirlpress

Other Books by Catherine Maven

- 101 Secrets of Canadian Culture
- **Bedtime Mindfulness** (Questions for Parents & Kids)

For Children:

- **Alien Animals Stole Our Alphabet** (rhyming - handwriting & alphabet book)
- **Alien Animals Coloring Book**
- **How to Train Your Puppy:** A READ-it-YOURSELF Guide for KIDS
- **The Cat in King Arthur's Cloak** (picture book)
- **'Magination Molly** (picture book)
- **Splash Toes Creek** (illustrator & publisher)

Novel

- **Coyote Summer** (YA fantasy novel)

What you can LEARN from this BOOK:

Let your puppy choose YOU!

Introduction

What do puppies need?

1. They need Love.
2. Puppies need good food.
3. Puppies need clean water.
4. Puppies need a place to pee and poop!
5. Puppies need a good place to sleep.
6. Puppies need PLAY!
7. Puppies need a BATH!
8. Puppies need FRIENDS!

What to TEACH your puppy

1. Teach your puppy not to NIP
2. Teach your puppy not to BARK all the time
3. Teach your puppy to "Come"
4. Some puppies can learn to "Fetch"
5. Teach your puppy to "Sit"
6. Teach your puppy to walk on a leash
7. Teach your puppy to go down stairs
8. Teach your puppy to "Shake a paw"

Conclusion

A Bit About Me

Let your puppy choose YOU!

NOTE: mixed breed dogs are generally healthier and live longer than purebred dogs. *Choose a RESCUE if you can! Lab mixes are good; husky mixes can be challenging!*

Sit with all the puppies and let one pick you.

Do you want a dog who **fetches**? Bring a small squeaky toy to toss. Your perfect puppy will fetch it naturally. Does the puppy drop it or does he growl and want to play Tug-of-War? *Choose one who will give you the ball!*

Do you want a **cuddly** dog? Sit on the floor. Which one climbs on you to lick your face?

Do you want a **therapy** dog? Some breeds of dog are better for support. **Google it!**

Do you want an **active** dog? One who loves to run and play? One who learns lots of **tricks**?

Or do you want a dog who is **relaxed** and **quiet**?

Choose a dog that suits your family. Google:
- *Active dogs*
- *Easy family dogs*
- *Dogs for first-time dog owners*
- *Hypoallergenic dogs*

Introduction:

Yay! You have picked your puppy! But how do you train her?

The most important thing to remember is that she is a BABY! She will sleep 18-20 hours a day when you first bring her home. She LOOKS like a TOY – but she's a BABY. You might want to play with her all the time. But let her sleep. She needs lots of sleep to grow and be happy. But when she wakes up, you can't ignore her, even if you're tired.

Remember: *She's part of your FAMILY now.*

What do puppies NEED?
Here are some things puppies need.

1. **Puppies need Love.** That's EASY.

Be gentle with your puppy. Give him cuddles and pet him!

Hold your puppy on your lap – if he is small. Your puppy needs lots and LOTS of attention and love.

2. Puppies need good food.

Don't feed your puppy "people" food. Cheese isn't good for her. (She'll get really smelly farts!) Most dogs just need kibble or a raw diet. Your vet can tell you what's best for your dog.

Healthy dog treats are okay. But wait until your puppy is about 4 months old.

3. Puppies need clean water.

Use a non-tipping dog dish.

Choose a metal dish. Wash it every day. Then fill it with fresh, cold water.

4. Puppies need a place to pee and poop!

Most puppies can start learning as soon as you bring them home. But they WILL have accidents!

Train your puppy to pee and poop outside. Or on a Puppy Pad.

Puppies don't remember what they did 5 minutes ago. So catch your puppy when she is just starting to pee or poop.

Pick her up and quickly take her outside to finish. Praise the puppy when she poops or pees outside. Tell her what a Good Girl she is!

MY FIRST PUPPY

Take your puppy outside about once an hour for the first few weeks. After that, take your puppy outside when he wakes up from a nap. Take your puppy outside when she finishes her food.

Soon he'll learn to "ask" to go out. He might whine at the door. Or just sit and stare at you! Show the puppy where to pee and poop. That's better than getting angry when he has an accident.

5. Puppies need a good place to sleep.

I recommend training your puppy to sleep in his crate.

Put an old t-shirt of yours in his bed so he feels safe. Cover the crate at night to help him sleep.

If she cries at night, you can stick your fingers through the bars, but don't let her out until morning.

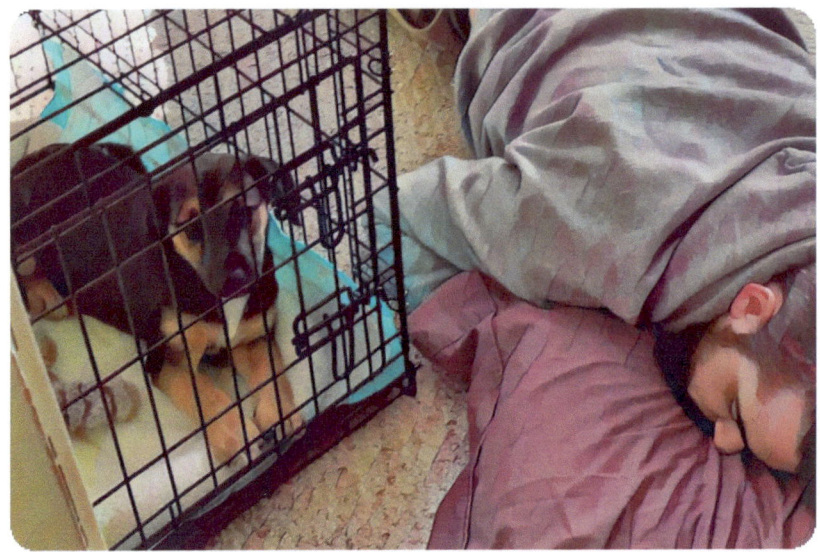

(Younger puppies might need to go out once at night to pee and poop. Your Mom or Dad can take them out.)

6. Puppies need PLAY!

Puppies are full of energy. They want to put everything in their mouth. Just like human babies!

Teach your puppy what they **can** play with.

Teach your puppy what they **can't** play with.

Some puppies chew things they shouldn't (like a shoe).

Take the shoe away and say, *"No!"* - but don't hit your puppy.

Give her a toy she CAN chew on.

Be **GENTLE**. This teaches your puppy that she can trust you.

If you hit her, she won't trust you. Remember, you are her *family* now!

7. Puppies need a BATH!

Start giving your puppy a regular bath when he is a baby.

Then he will enjoy getting a bath when he's bigger. Use a short hose and warm *(NOT hot!)* water.

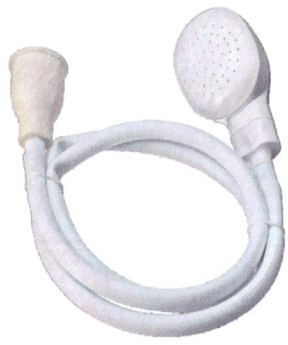

8. Puppies need FRIENDS!

Wait until your puppy has all of her vaccinations. Then start introducing her to other puppies to make friends.

Your puppy needs to learn to be a good friend to other dogs. Puppies sometimes play rough. But that's okay, as long as they aren't crying. If your puppy runs back to you, pet her but don't pick her up unless the other dog is hurting her.

Your local leash-free park might have a Puppy Park or a Small Dog Park.

That's a good place to start. Bigger dogs might be too strong for your puppy. You don't want them to scare him. Or hurt him.

Things to TEACH Your Puppy

Teach your Puppy to be GOOD

1. Teach your Puppy not to NIP!

If your puppy nips or bites you, say *"OW!"* as loudly as you can! Then say *"NO!"*

Your puppy is just playing. He doesn't mean to hurt you. Puppies nip each other when they play. But teach him it's *not* okay to nip **you!** **(But DON'T hit him – give him a toy he can chew on instead.)**

2. Teach your puppy NOT to BARK all the time

Puppies bark for a number of reasons. Maybe she's afraid of something. Like a noise, a person, or another animal. Maybe she's bored. She's asking you to play with her. Maybe she's lonely.

Don't YELL at her. To her, that sounds like BARKING, and she will bark MORE!

If your puppy is afraid, pick her up. Hold her and tell her she's okay. Pet her. When she stops barking, give her a treat.

If your puppy is bored or lonely, play with him. But not right away.

If you play with him every time he barks, he will bark more often. *Ignore him for a few seconds or minutes.*

Your puppy is never too young to start to learn a couple of TRICKS!

3. A trick every puppy can learn is "Come".

Sit on the floor. When your puppy is several feet away, tap your lap and call, "Come!" Use his or her name.

My dog is Kiju, so I say, "*Come*, Kiju!"

When she comes, give her lots of love. Tell her she's a Good Girl (or Good Boy). Practice with short distances and then longer and longer ones (in your back yard or at a leash-free park). Give her a treat when she returns to you. I can take my dogs to a large park with no fences because I know they will come when I call.

4. Teach Your Puppy to FETCH.

Some puppies are born with a natural wish to fetch. That means, go get a toy or ball and bring it back to you.

(My puppy was fetching at 7 weeks. But most are a bit older.)

Not every dog will fetch. Some dogs really enjoy it. But some dogs don't enjoy it. If your puppy won't fetch, don't get angry. She is just being herself!

5. Teach Your Puppy to SIT.

The next trick your puppy can learn is "Sit."

Make sure your puppy is looking in your eyes. Puppies need to look at you to listen to you.

Say, "Sit". He won't sit at first. Gently push his behind down. Keep saying, "Sit." When the puppy sits, give him more love (and maybe a treat)!

6. Teach Your Puppy to walk on a leash

First of all, use a harness, *not* a collar.

This is how I taught my puppy to walk on a leash. I walked as far away as the leash let me. Then I crouched down and called her name. "***Come,*** Kiju." When she came, I gave her love. Then I walked away as far as the leash let me again. And called her to Come. I did this over and over for a few minutes per day. She might not want to learn this right away. The most important thing to remember is to **be patient**.

Don't drag her! She's not a toy. She's alive, and she's a baby. She will learn, but many babies learn s-l-o-w-l-y. Soon she will start trotting beside you!

7. Teach your puppy to go down stairs.

(Going up stairs is usually easier and requires little training.)

Put your puppy on the very last step – the bottom stair. Then call him or use a treat to get him to go down one stair.

Repeat, one stair at a time, each time you need him to go down stairs. Don't try to teach this all in one day.

Be patient! If you force him to do too much, he'll end up afraid of stairs.

So, one stair the first time.

Two stairs the second time.

Three stairs the third time.

And so on.

Soon he will be taking the stairs like a PRO!

8. Teach Your Puppy to Shake a Paw

Your puppy can learn to shake a paw!

After your puppy will sit on command, tell him to sit. Then gently lift up one of his paws. Say, "Shake a paw!" and smile. You can give the puppy a treat now. Then put his paw down. Move to a different spot. Tell him, "Sit." Lift his paw and say, "Shake a paw!" again and smile. You can give the puppy another treat now.

Do this 2 or 3 more times, then stop for today. But do this a few times a day, every day for 2 weeks. Repetition is the key to training your puppy.

Remember: A minute or two of training is all your puppy can learn at one time. Then *STOP!*

Play with your puppy, hug your puppy. After a few weeks, (or sooner!) your puppy will start to lift his paw when you say, "Shake a paw!"

Conclusion:

These are just some ideas to help you *start* learning how to train your puppy. I recommend taking your puppy for **Obedience Lessons.** But if you can't, YouTube has lots of good videos to help you. There are many good books and websites, too. **Remember**: Puppies want our love very much. So when you reward a good puppy with love, she is VERY happy!

Enjoy your puppy. Both of you have lots to learn!

A Bit About Me:

Kiju & me, Oct. 2020

I wrote my first short story when I was seven years old. While in university, I wrote a weekly humor column for the *McMaster Silhouette* newspaper and won some prizes for my writing. I used to work as a newspaper reporter.

I have had dogs (and some cats) all of my life. I took each dog for obedience training and learned that the owner is the one who needs training! Dogs really WANT to do the right thing. It is up to us to teach them what we want them to do – and what we DON'T want them to do.

I am a mother of 3 boys. I taught my kids to train our puppies with LOVE (& treats). When we bond with our puppy, he will do anything for us. If we train our puppy right, she will be a good member of the family and a good member of society.

I'm also a visual artist who sells paintings and handmade jewelry. I have just started illustrating my own books, using a digital watercolor collage technique.

Thanks for reading!
- **Catherine Maven, M.A.**

@catherinemavenart

catherinemaven.blogspot.com

www.ingramcontent.com/pod-product-compliance
Lightning Source LLC
Chambersburg PA
CBHW041808040426
42449CB00001B/14